Fifth Word and Nottingham Playhouse
in association with Brixton House

SONALI BHATTACHARYYA

LIBERATION SQUARES

T0352923

Liberation Squares was first performed in the Neville Studio at
Nottingham Playhouse, on 12 April 2024.

LIBERATION SQUARES

BY SONALI BHATTACHARYYA

Ruqaya	**Vaneeka Dadhria**
Sabi	**Asha Hassan**
Xara	**Halema Hussain**

Other parts played by members of the company.

Director	**Milli Bhatia**
Designer	**Tomás Palmer**
Lighting Designer	**Joshua Gadsby**
Composer and Sound Designer	**Elena Peña**
Movement Director	**Iskandar إسكندر R. Sharazuddin**
Casting Director	**Arthur Carrington**
Dramaturg	**afshan d'souza-lodhi**
Assistant Director	**Jade Franks**
Associate Designer	**Ania Levy**
Associate Sound Designer	**Bella Kear**
Costume Supervisor	**Emilie Carter**
Props Supervisor	**Hannah Zemlak**
Production Managers	**Rachel Bowen**
	Andrew Quick
	Jamie Smith
Stage Manager	**Katie Bosomworth**
	Chloe Chancheong

Vaneeka Dadhria | Ruqaya

Vaneeka graduated from St Mary's University, Twickenham in 2019 with a BA in Drama & Theatre Arts. She is an actress, beatboxer, songwriter & all round creative. Vaneeka also leads Beatboxing/Theatre Workshops and has worked alongside Ambassador Theatre Group, The Tottenham Hotspur Foundation and schools across the UK.

Credits include: *Cyrano De Bergerac* (West End's Playhouse Theatre, Harold Pinter Theatre, Theatre Royal Glasgow, BAM Brooklyn) and *Unite – It's Not As Simple As Black & White, The Lucky Mother Summons Francis Galton, I just Needed Cash* (The New Vic, Stoke).

Asha Hassan | Sabi

East Londoner Asha is best known for her series regular role in BBC Three comedy *Bad Education*. She made her professional screen debut in the multi award-winning feature film *Rocks*. Other screen credits include the title role in the Film4 short *Salma*, produced by Slam Films (Stephen Mangan and Louise Delamere) which follows a teenager living in Grenfell Tower. On stage Asha starred in the two-hander *Cuttin' It* at Manchester's Royal Exchange Theatre for which she was widely praised. She has recently completed work on a drama series for Disney+ from an acclaimed writer and director.

Halema Hussain | Xara

TV credits include: new ITV comedy series for transmission summer 2024; *Horrible Histories*, BBC 2023; *Dreamland*, SKY 2022; *We Are Lady Parts*, CH4 2021; *Doctors*, BBC 2021; *Casualty*, BBC 2021.

Films include: *Supernova*, (BBC & BFI); *Mo <3 Kyra 4Eva* (Film4).

Theatre credits include: *The Father and the Assassin* (National Theatre); *Vardy vs Rooney: The Wagatha Christie Trial* (ELP Productions/Ambassador Theatre); *Dawaat* (Tara Theatre); *Aaliyah After Antigone* (Freedom Studio); *Does My Bomb Look Big in This?* (Soho Theatre).

Sonali Bhattacharyya | Writer

Sonali Bhattacharyya is an award-winning playwright and screenwriter (Sonia Friedman Production Award and Theatre Uncut Political Playwriting Award for *Chasing Hares*). Her play *King Troll (The Fawn)* was a finalist for the Women's Prize for Playwriting.

Her plays include *The Jungle Book* (Chichester Festival Theatre); *Arabian Nights* (Bristol Old Vic); *Chasing Hares* (Young Vic and Theatre Uncut); *Two Billion Beats* (Orange Tree Theatre); *Two Billion Beats* (Korean translation, Kirkos Theatre, Seoul); *Silence* (Tara Theatre and Donmar Warehouse); *Megaball* (National Theatre Learning); *Slummers*

(Cardboard Citizens/Bunker Theatre); *The Invisible Boy* (Kiln Theatre) and *Assembly: The Teachers' Play* and *2066* (Almeida Theatre).

Sonali is a graduate of the Royal Court Writers' Group, the Old Vic 12, and Donmar Warehouse's Future Forms Programme.

She is part of the writing team for new television drama The Split Up from Sister Pictures/BBC, and is currently under commission to the Bristol Old Vic, Cardboard Citizens and Kali Theatre/New Diorama Theatre.

Milli Bhatia | Director

Milli (she/her) is a Theatre, Film and Radio Director, and Dramaturg from East London. She is an Associate Artist at Synergy.

She was Associate Director at The Royal Court, Associate Artist at The Bush Theatre, Resident Assistant Director at Birmingham Rep and Creative Associate at The Gate Theatre. Her training includes The National Theatre Director's Programme, and The Old Vic 12.

She is a two-time Olivier Award nominee, for her productions of *seven methods of killing kylie jenner* and *Blue Mist*, both premiered at The Royal Court Theatre.

Her work as Director includes: *Blue Mist* by Mohamed-Zain Dada (Royal Court), *seven methods of killing kylie jenner* by

Jasmine Lee-Jones (Jerwood Theatre Upstairs 2019, Jerwood Theatre Downstairs 2021, Film 2022, Public Theater New York and Woolly Mammoth Washington DC 2023, Royal Court), *seven methods of killing kylie jenner* (Swedish language production) (Riksteatern, Swedish National Theatre, National tour 2022. Selected to return for the Biennale, Dramaten in 2023), *Chasing Hares* by Sonali Bhattacharyya (Young Vic), *Maryland* by Lucy Kirkwood (co director, Royal Court/South Bank Centre), *My White Best Friend and other letters left unsaid* (Bunker 2018/2019, Royal Court 2020), *Dismantle This Room* by Nina Segal (Bush Theatre/transferred to Royal Court), *Baghdaddy* by Jasmine Naziha Jones (Royal Court), *This Liquid Earth* by Amy Jephta (Royal Court/Edinburgh International Festival), *HomeBODY* by Jasmine Lee-Jones (Young Vic), *Yash Gill's Power Half Hour* by Nikesh Shukla, *The Hijabi Monologues* (Bush Theatre), *Living Newspaper* (Royal Court), *Ghosts In The Blood* by Joel Tan (Audible).

Tomás Palmer | Designer

Tomás Palmer is an artist and designer who works across theatre, dance, opera and performance art. Tomás trained at the Glasgow School of Art and the Royal Welsh College of Music and Drama. He is a 2021 Linbury prize for theatre design recipient and was the production designer on the BAFTA and BIFA Award-winning short film *Too Rough* in 2022.

As an artist, he has created installations/performance pieces for the Centre for Contemporary Arts (Glasgow), Transmission Gallery (Glasgow) and Embassy Gallery (Edinburgh).

Set and costume design credits include: *Dreaming and Drowning* (Bush Theatre); *Blue Mist* (Royal Court); *The Bacchae* (Lyric Hammersmith); *My Uncle Is Not Pablo Escobar* (Brixton House); *Sanctuary* (Access All Areas); Sophocles' *Oedipus/Silent Practice* (LAMDA); *The Wellspring* [co-design with Rosie Elnile] (Royal and Derngate, Northampton); *Time Is Running Out* (Gate Theatre, Cardiff); *Winning* (Glasgow School of Art); *Autocue* (Centre for Contemporary Art Glasgow).

Costume design credits include *Julius Caesar* [co-costume design with Rosanna Vize] (RSC) and *Multiple Casualty Incident* (Yard Theatre).

Joshua Gadsby | Lighting Designer

Joshua is a Lighting Designer and creative collaborator working across theatre, dance and live art. He regularly co-designs set, costume, and lighting with designer Naomi Kuyck-Cohen.

Lighting Designs include: *Kiss Marry Kill* (Dante or Die, UK Tour); *Dreaming and Drowning* (Bush Theatre); *New Beginning* (Queen's Theatre Hornchurch); *Mom, How Did You Meet the Beatles* (CFT); *Who Killed My Father* (Tron & UK Tour); *The Beauty Queen of Leenane* (Theatre by the Lake); *Alice in Wonderland* (Mercury Theatre, Colchester); *Gulliver's Travels* (lighting co-design, Unicorn Theatre), *Robin Hood: Legend Of The Forgotten Forest* (Bristol Old Vic); *Cat on a Hot Tin Roof* (Leicester Curve and ETT Tour); *in a word* (Young Vic); *A Kettle of Fish* (The Yard); *The Tyler Sisters*, *Alligators* (Hampstead Theatre); *Still Ill* (New Diorama/Kandinksy); *As We Like It, Dragging Words, In Good Company* (The Place); *RISE: Macro vs. Micro* (Old Vic New Voices).

Co-designs include: *The Winston Machine* (New Diorama); *There Is A Light That Never Goes Out: Scenes From The Luddite Rebellion* (Royal Exchange Manchester); *Trainers* (The Gate); *Dinomania* (New Diorama) and *Trap Street* (New Diorama and Schaubühne, Berlin) both for Kandinsky theatre.

Elena Peña | Composer and Sound Designer

Elena's recent theatre credits include: *Cinderella* (Brixton House), *The Magic Finger* (Unicorn Theatre), *Blue Mist* (Royal Court Theatre; Olivier Award nomination 2024 – Outstanding achievement in affiliate theatre), *As You Like It* (Royal Shakespeare Company), *Wuthering Heights*

(China Plate/UK Tour); *Songs Across the Sueniverse* (Sherman Theatre), *Misty* (The Shed, NYC), *Baghdaddy* (Royal Court Theatre), *seven methods of killing kylie jenner* (Royal Court Theatre and Riksteatern, Sweden), *Silence* (Donmar Warehouse & Tara Theatre), *The Darkest Part of the Night* (Kiln Theatre); *two Palestinians go dogging* (Royal Court Theatre); *Nora: A Doll's House* (Royal Exchange Theatre). Co-designed with Pete Malkin, *The Chairs* (Almeida Theatre); *Trouble in Mind* (National Theatre); *Maryland* (Royal Court Theatre); *Rockets and Blue Lights* (National Theatre & Royal Exchange Theatre – OnComm Award for Best Audio Production).

Elena is an Associate Artist at Inspector Sands.

Iskandar إسكندر **R. Sharazuddin |** Movement Director

Iskandar إسكندر R. Sharazuddin is a British-Bruneian theatre artist and creative producer. He is an Associate at Headlong Theatre and the Joint Artistic Director of Ellandar Productions, a British East and Southeast Asian (BESEA) company producing work focused on Asian diaspora and British Muslim narratives & writers.

Iskandar is the Resident Director and Puppetry Captain on *My Neighbour Totoro* (RSC, Studio Ghibli, Barbican) and in 2023 directed the first all East &

Southeast Asian company of Puccini's *Turandot* for Grimeborn Opera Festival at Arcola Theatre – Winner of the Off West End Award for Opera Performance and nominated for Best Opera Production. He works as a director and movement director, selected credits as movement director include: *The Bleeding Tree* (Southwark Playhouse); *harmony.* 天人合一 (York Theatre Royal/The Pleasance); *Garden of Words* (Whole Hog Theatre/Park Theatre); *Blackout Songs* (Hampstead Theatre – nominated for an Olivier Award for Achievement in an Affiliate Theatre); *Worth* (New Earth Theatre & Chester Storyhouse); and *Così fan tutte* & *Satyagraha* (English National Opera 2021–22 Season in collaboration with Improbable). He was the Dance Captain/Resident on *How To Train Your Dragon: Live* (Dreamworks SKG, World Tour, National Broadway) and the Associate Movement Director on *The Climbers* (Theatre By The Lake). His dance-theatre work co-conceived with Iona Kirk, *(un)written • (un)heard* was awarded the International Dance & Physical Theatre Award at Fringe World Festival Western Australia 2020.

Iskandar is also an award-winning writer and a recipient of the Tony Craze Playwriting Award from Soho Theatre. He has been long-listed for the Bruntwood

Playwriting Prize and shortlisted for the Off West End Adopt a Playwright Award. Selected playwriting credits include: *i must go in, the fog is rising* (Arcola Theatre); *The Apologists* (VAULT Festival, Omnibus Theatre, and the Old 505 – Nominated for a Sydney Theatre Award); *Post-Mortem* (Assembly Festival Edinburgh 2019, The Blue Room Theatre Western Australia, and Holden Street Theatres, Adelaide Festival) and *Silently Hoping* (VAULT Festival & Applecart Arts).

Arthur Carrington | Casting Director

As Casting Director, theatre includes: *Bluets, Mates in Chelsea, Blue Mist, Hope has a Happy Meal, Black Superhero, Graceland, Jews. In Their Own Words, That Is Not Who I Am, two Palestinians go dogging, The Glow, A Fight Against…, Maryland, Poet in da Corner* (Royal Court); *The Contingency Plan* (Sheffield Crucible); *Barefoot in the Park* (Pitlochry Festival Theatre/Royal Lyceum); *Returning to Haifa* (Finborough Theatre); *The Ugly One* (Park Theatre); *The Mountaintop* (Young Vic).

As Casting Associate, theatre includes: *The Hills of California* (Harold Pinter Theatre); *Macbeth* (UK/US Tour); *Lyonesse* (Harold Pinter Theatre); *La Cage Aux Folles* (Regents Park Open Air Theatre); *The Pillowman* (Duke of York's Theatre); *Hamnet* (RSC/Garrick Theatre); *Drive Your Plow Over the Bones of the Dead* (Complicité, UK/European tour); *Jerusalem* (Apollo Theatre); *Leopoldstadt* (Wyndham's Theatre); *Uncle Vanya* (Harold Pinter Theatre); *The Night of the Iguana* (Noel Coward Theatre); *Rosmersholm* (Duke of York's Theatre); *True West* (Vaudeville Theatre); *The Ferryman* (Royal Court/Gielgud Theatre/Bernard B. Jacobs Theatre, New York); *Shipwreck, Albion* (Almeida Theatre); *A Very, Very, Very Dark Matter* (Bridge Theatre); *Hangmen* (Royal Court/Wyndham's Theatre/Atlantic Theatre Company, New York).

Film includes: *The Unlikely Pilgrimage of Harold Fry, Maryland, Ballywalter*.

afshan d'souza-lodhi | Dramaturg

afshan d'souza-lodhi was born in Dubai and forged in Manchester. She is a writer of scripts and poetry. Her work has been performed and translated into numerous languages across the world. afshan has been writer-in-residence for Sky Studios, New Writing North, Royal Exchange Theatre, Warner Bros Discovery and was writer-in-residence for Bluebird Pictures. afshan was also one of the first to receive The National Theatre's Peter Shaffer award in 2022.

afshan has been a BAFTA BFI Flare mentee and has developed a TV series with Sky Studios. A

TV pilot she wrote called Chop Chop, was selected for the second annual #MuslimList (The Black List).

As well as her own writing, afshan is keen to develop other younger and emerging artists and sits on the boards of Manchester Literature Festival, Pie Radio and Royal Exchange Theatre Manchester. She is also the WGGB Regional chair of Manchester and Lancashire.

www.afshandl.com
Social media: @afshandl

Jade Franks | Assistant Director

Jade Franks is a theatremaker and actor from Liverpool. The inclusion and celebration of work from and for working class people is vital to Jade's creative process. She believes that the work that goes into building and maintaining relationships with the communities in the audience is as important as the work that goes into creating the shows themselves. Jade is currently

Outreach Manager on *For Black Boys Who Have Considered Suicide When The Hue Gets Too Heavy* by Ryan Calais Cameron at The Garrick Theatre. Previous directing credits include assisting Vicky Featherstone at The Royal Court and The Liverpool Everyman on *Cuckoo* by Michael Wynne.

Acting credits include: *Hot in Here* (Gate Theatre); *One Night Stand* (Royal Court); *Maryland* (Royal Court/Battersea Arts Center for WOW Festival); *Run, Painkiller, Slambition* (Theatre Royal, Stratford East).

NOTTINGHAM PLAYHOUSE

Nottingham Playhouse is dedicated to making bold and thrilling world-class theatre, proudly made in Nottingham. In 2023, it was named the UK's Most Welcoming Theatre in the UK Theatre Awards.

Nottingham Playhouse is one of the country's leading producing theatres, renowned for creating ambitious and diverse productions, many of which have toured across the UK and have transferred to the West End and Broadway.

The theatre's acclaimed participation programme creates life-changing experiences for the local community and its Theatre of Sanctuary status ensures it is a space where everyone feels they belong. Nottingham Playhouse nurtures the next generation of theatre-makers through their dynamic artist support programme, Amplify.

Recently awarded a Silver Carbon Literacy standard, Nottingham Playhouse is committed to continually improving its sustainability standards across productions and its Grade II* listed building.

For more information about Nottingham Playhouse visit **www.nottinghamplayhouse.co.uk**

Chief Executive **Stephanie Sirr**
Artistic Director **Adam Penford**

Fifth Word are an award-winning theatre company based in the East Midlands, founded in 2007. They develop and produce vital new plays that change how people see the world. They make work with and for younger audiences (age 14–25) and under-served communities: uncovering the stories that need to be told.

Their shows tour across the UK. Fifth Word productions are always powerful, bold and accessible: amplifying the stories of those who often go unheard or easily slip through the cracks in society. Fifth Word collaborate with a range of communities who do not always see the arts as for them: empowering them to tell their own stories through different artistic means. Fifth Word's community projects connect closely with their productions; everything they do is driven by the desire to foster creative ambition, develop new talent, and platform under-represented voices.

They are passionate about contributing to a strong new writing culture in the Midlands, and helping to discover and develop the next generation of talented playwrights in the region. They produce plays by the most exciting playwrights of the moment, both from the Midlands and from across the UK. They develop a thoughtful, rigorous, and bespoke process with each writer they work with, to ensure that these stories reach the stage in their full power.

Fifth Word's recent productions include the world premiere of *We Need New Names,* adapted by Mufaro Makubika from the Booker Prize-shortlisted novel by NoViolet Bulawayo (a co-production with New Perspectives in association with Brixton House); the world premiere of *Lava* by James Fritz (a co-production with Nottingham Playhouse); and the world premiere of *All the Little Lights* by Jane Upton (a co-production with Nottingham Playhouse), joint winner of the George Devine Award.

fifthword.co.uk

Artistic Director	**Laura Ford**
Producer	**Corinne Salisbury**
Engagement Producer	**Zahra Butt**
Assistant Producer	**Kate Spencer**
Digital Communications Associate	**Daljinder Johal**
Tour Marketing	**Eragona Communications**

LIBERATION SQUARES

Sonali Bhattacharyya

'If I didn't define myself for myself, I would be crunched into other people's fantasies for me and eaten alive.'

Audre Lorde

Author's Note

I wanted to write a play about the incredible imagination, inquisitiveness and creativity teenagers have – this is what forges the messy bond between Xara, Ruqaya and Sabi. Right now, we're witnessing rapidly normalised Islamophobia and racism, including in government policies like the Prevent surveillance programme, and I wanted to explore how this inhibits young people's confidence, freedom of expression, and even their futures. I wanted to tell this story through the points of view of young people themselves, with all of the joyful spirit of rebellion that entails.

Sonali Bhattacharyya

Characters

SABI, *introvert, overthinker, big on details*
RUQAYA, *extrovert, loose talker, richly imaginative*
XARA, *charismatic, articulate, confident but lonely*

All British Muslim girls in their teens

NADIA, *articulate and polished course leader. To be played by any/all of the three actors*

This text went to press before the end of rehearsals and so may differ slightly from the play as performed.

Prologue

RUQAYA *and* SABI *enter and put together what they need to tell us this story. They write the locations where the story will take place on a whiteboard.* RUQAYA *beatboxes, establishing a different soundscape for each location.*

SABI (*direct address*). You've all heard a hundred different versions of what happened. We're here to tell you how it *really* went down… Hard to believe this all started just a few months ago. A lot's happened in the meantime.

RUQAYA (*direct address*). Yeah. Like I got *sick* at beatboxing…

Scene One

A few months ago. RUQAYA *and* SABI *enter in their school uniforms, rapping and dancing, with a carefully choreographed routine.* RUQAYA *is the more confident of the two and* SABI *has to sneak looks at her every now and then to make sure she's getting the moves right. It's the afternoon and they're in Ruqaya's bedroom.*

RUQAYA. Ruqaya and Sabi, we're here to *disarm,*

SABI. Leave your preconceptions at the door, yeah?

RUQAYA. We're sounding the alarm.

SABI. Putting forward our case in the public eye.

RUQAYA. Leaving the shadows. We're ready to fly.

SABI. Fly, fly, fly, fly, fly.

RUQAYA. I'm not a ninja, I'm the harbinger of justice and truth,
No need to be aloof.

SABI *slows down. Misses part of the routine.*

My eyes are open, my tongue is sharp,
So get with the programme cos we're hitting the mark.

SABI (*breaking out of the routine completely*). When did we add those?

RUQAYA. Last night. Was almost asleep. It's like they came to me in my dreams, yeah? You know Kendrick Lamar comes up with lyrics like that?

SABI. You're not Kendrick Lamar.

RUQAYA. I'm just saying. I'm literally coming up with this stuff *in my sleep*.

SABI. I don't like it.

RUQAYA. Why?

SABI. We're not saying we're 'ninjas'. I'm not saying that.

RUQAYA. The line is 'I'm *not* a ninja'.

SABI. Yeah, but we say it and it puts the idea in people's minds, doesn't it?

RUQAYA. Dunno, does it?

SABI. It's like saying – 'don't think about elephants'. And then all you can think about is elephants.

RUQAYA. Didn't say we were like elephants.

SABI. Yeah, but we're not like ninjas either, are we?

RUQAYA. I am.

SABI. No you're not.

RUQAYA. Ninjas are *brilliant*. They hide out in underground lairs and kill people with swords and you never know they're coming, you just see the flash of their eyes as they plunge you into oblivion. (*Mimes dying in agony.*) You love ninjas.

SABI. No I don't.

RUQAYA. Used to.

SABI. I don't any more.

RUQAYA. Ninjas are the closest thing we've ever had to real life superheroes. If Moon Girl was a real person she'd be a ninja.

SABI. What…?

RUQAYA. Or Ms. Marvel. If Kamala Khan was real she'd be a ninja.

SABI. She's not real, and ninjas aren't real.

RUQAYA. They're more real than your comic books, that's all I'm saying.

SABI. What if Zoe or Steph see this? Or the girls from St Saviour's?

RUQAYA. How would they see it? You never let us record anything.

SABI. They might hear about it.

RUQAYA. From *who*?

SABI. Not giving them ammunition to throw at us.

RUQAYA. We could stir up beef and get people to follow us. People love a bit of aggro. They'll all want a ringside seat.

SABI. No one cares who we have beef with.

RUQAYA. Not *yet*.

SABI. …And even if they did. They're not going to be there for us when we're getting the bus home, are they?

RUQAYA. Steph and those bitches wouldn't mess with us if we had bare followers.

SABI. You are dreaming, Ruqaya.

RUQAYA. 'I'm not a ninja, I'm the harbinger of truth…' Don't care what you say, that rhyme slaps.

SABI. We can't say things just because they rhyme.

RUQAYA. A rhyme makes sense. A rhyme is natural. A rhyme flows –

   ''Tis light makes colour visible: at night
   Red, greene, and russet vanish from thy sight.'

SABI....Okay.

RUQAYA. It's Rumi.

SABI. I *know*. I get it. Still not saying that line.

RUQAYA. Okay, relax, it's not that deep. I'll change it. Told you, lyrics are bare easy for me anyway.

SABI. *Thank* you.

RUQAYA. You messed up the steps after the second line.

SABI. No I didn't.

RUQAYA. You're supposed to take one step out. Otherwise we're not symmetrical.

SABI. We said two steps.

RUQAYA. Yeah, well maybe *you* need two, because of your short legs. (*Direct address.*) We always did a knee bend, arm out, hip swivel, and a floor touch.

SABI (*direct address*). It worked, for that song. For the chorus.

RUQAYA (*direct address*). For the verse it was more of a freestyle.

SABI (*direct address*). Not me. I always did a step left, step right, step forwards, lunge, arms out, head turn.

   She runs through the moves in the moment, efficient, concentrating.

   Ruqaya's thing was always hip hop – the music, the lyrics, the videos, everything.

RUQAYA (*direct address*). Sabi's thing was comics.

SABI (*direct address*). *Graphic novels*.

RUQAYA (*direct address*). And being a tight arse.

SABI (*direct address*). Before Xara, it was just me and Ruqaya. Things were simple. Straightforward. We had a system.

RUQAYA (*direct address*). It's called being tac-tic-*al*.

SABI (*direct address*). We had to get the bus to and from school twice a day. Keeping our heads down was just best for our mental health.

RUQAYA (*direct address*). Defence was the best form of *of*fence.

Scene Two

They wheel out a whiteboard and SABI *draws a diagram*.

RUQAYA (*direct address*). Stop BD was nearer to both of us.

SABI (*direct address*). But we used the one further down, like, five minutes away. Stop BE.

SABI *draws the two of them at the bus stop*. RUQAYA *takes the pen from* SABI *and amends one of the stick figures she's drawn*. SABI *gives her a look*.

RUQAYA (*to* SABI). What? I'm taller than you. (*Direct address*.) Thing about that stop, BE, is you could see *all* the way up to the Co-op.

SABI (*direct address*). To Stop BD.

RUQAYA (*direct address*). Where Steph and that lot got on.

SABI (*direct address*). So if we saw them…

RUQAYA (*direct address*). We knew to stay put instead. Kill time.

SABI (*direct address*). Maybe chill at the library for a bit.

RUQAYA (*direct address*). We could until it became '*Bibliotek*'.

SABI (*direct address*). In quotation marks.

RUQAYA (*direct address*). With a K.

SABI (*direct address*). It even means 'library'. Taking the pee, right?

RUQAYA (*direct address*). They have organic cokes in glass bottles for *four* pounds.

SABI (*direct address*). And you have to *rent* desk space. Maybe that's why *ten* thousand people signed the petition to stop them shutting the library down.

RUQAYA (*direct address*). Did they listen?

Sardonic laughter. They both put on rucksacks and they're at the bus stop, several weeks ago.

Hey, know what I heard?

SABI. What?

RUQAYA. You're allowed *off site* for lunch at Everyman College. For real.

SABI.…Wow. That's mad.

RUQAYA. That's mad? No, *this* is mad. *Super Extra Bubble Tea* is just ten minutes' walk away. Looked it up on Google Maps. You know what that means?

SABI.…Bubble Tea at lunchtime…?

RUQAYA. Not just any bubble tea – Super Extra Bubble Tea, Sabi, you know that's the best place in like the whole south-east, they won an award and everything? Ten minutes there, ten minutes back, that means we'll have a whole twenty minutes, and I'm talking lychee, I'm talking chocolate Oreo, I'm talking a watermelon martini mocktail in the summer when we're feeling cheeky. And we won't have to worry about Steph, or Stop BE, or the size of our umbrellas *ever again*.

RUQAYA *holds up her hand for a high-five.* SABI *dutifully responds.*

It's just over a hundred sleeps away, Sabi. You can taste that ice-blended goodness right now, can't you? Right?

SABI. Um...

RUQAYA. We got this, you know it.

SABI. Ruqs, I've got to talk to you about something... You know I couldn't come over last week?

RUQAYA. For taco night?

SABI. Yeah, for taco night.

RUQAYA. You missed last week too.

SABI. I'll make it up to you.

RUQAYA. Did it heat up okay, though?

SABI. It was nice. Tell your mum thank you.

RUQAYA. Still tasty? Not too dry?

SABI. No, not at all.

RUQAYA. Wasn't too spicy for you? Thought it might be too spicy.

SABI. I can take my spice.

RUQAYA. Er, yeah, okay, if you say so.

SABI. I need to tell you what I was really doing.

RUQAYA. Bus is coming. Can't see them... Nah, there they are. They're getting on.

RUQAYA *quickly puts up her umbrella.* SABI *roots around in her rucksack for hers.*

Come on.

SABI. Can't find my umbrella...

RUQAYA. It's indicating.

SABI. Must've left it at home.

RUQAYA. Stop joking around.

SABI. I'm not…

RUQAYA. Fuck's sake…

> RUQAYA *pulls her close. They huddle under* RUQAYA*'s small umbrella.*

SABI. You've brought this titchy one out, again? Barely keep your shoulders dry.

RUQAYA. The others were eight ninety-nine.

SABI. It's coming…

> *They huddle closer.*

(*Direct address.*) There was always a queue at BE. We were soft targets.

RUQAYA (*direct address*). And that morning there was this old guy asking if the bus went to the leisure centre.

SABI (*direct address*). And the driver was like 'which leisure centre?'

RUQAYA (*direct address*). And the man was like 'the big one'.

SABI (*direct address*). My guy had literally *no* idea what was at stake.

RUQAYA. What were you saying?

SABI. It doesn't matter now…

RUQAYA. Your eye's twitching.

> SABI *tries to cover her eye as they brace themselves. A window on the top deck opens and a shower of phlegm and various coke cans and crisp packets is emitted from above. The bus stops.*

Oh shit, it's here. Get your keys out.

> RUQAYA *holds her keys between her fingers like a weapon.*

If they try anything just go Wolverine on their ass.

SABI (*fumbling with her keys*). Like this…?

RUQAYA. *No*. Fuck's sake, Sabi.

> RUQAYA *tries to help her. The doors open.* XARA *gets off. Stunned beat. The bus pulls away.*

XARA (*of the keys*). Those for me?

RUQAYA. No.

> RUQAYA*'s jaw drops.*

> (*Direct address.*) At that moment, *everything changed*. Xara Hussein, the one and only, in *our* ends? *What* the actual… [fuck]?! She had, like, twenty *thousand* followers on Insta.

SABI (*direct address*). And every single one of them could smell her perfume.

RUQAYA (*direct address*). Never, in my whole life, had I breathed the same air as someone, you know… famous? I mean, Mum took me to an in-store appearance by Harry Styles once but he was two hours late and we had to get back to pick up my sister so we missed him. But here she was, standing right in front of us. 'It's your girl Xara!' The actual baddest bitch from the internet at *our* stop, BE? Oh. My. Days.

SABI (*direct address*). She looked a lot taller on TikTok.

RUQAYA (*direct address*). She put these sick videos out about a different fierce queen every week. I recognised her straightaway.

SABI (*direct address*). So did I, but wasn't about to say where we'd met, was I?

> RUQAYA *motions to* SABI *to put away their keys.*

RUQAYA (*to* XARA). What did you say to them?

XARA. The dirty little skets spitting out the window? Just went over and shut it.

RUQAYA. You just went… over…?

XARA. Yeah.

RUQAYA *and* SABI *are lost for words.*

RUQAYA (*direct address*). That's when I knew we were going to be fam. For life.

SABI *doesn't agree but bites her tongue.*

(*Direct address*). She moved here from the buzzing metropolitan chocolate city of *Bristol*. (*To* XARA.) I'm Ruqaya.

XARA. Hiya Ruqaya.

RUQAYA *laughs, a bit too loud.*

RUQAYA. Good one. This is Sabi. Say hello, Sabi.

SABI. Hello.

XARA. Hi.

RUQAYA (*to* XARA). Oh my days, you go Heathcote Secondary too?!

XARA (*of her uniform*). Just started. But I've decided not to go in today.

SABI. Why?

XARA. New TikTok challenge just dropped. Haven't I met you before?

SABI. No.

RUQAYA (*to* XARA). Do you go comic club too?

XARA. *No.*

SABI. You've got me mixed up with someone else.

RUQAYA. *Love* your videos. My favourite's the one you did about that spy woman? Blew. My. Mind. Must have watched it like, fifty times.

SABI. *Ruqaya…*

XARA. Aw, you're so sweet.

RUQAYA. Where do you get your ideas from? No way I could do that.

XARA. Course you could. Everyone's got something to say. You just need to step up and speak your truth.

RUQAYA. You really think so?

XARA. Of course. You're a creative, outspoken sister, right?

RUQAYA. Hundred per cent.

XARA. And... (*Of* SABI.) You... Want to come shoot this video?

RUQAYA. *Us?* Yeah, for sure, let's go.

SABI. What about school?

XARA. You're going to learn a lot more than *at school*.

RUQAYA. Yeah, exactly, Sabi.

XARA. You coming then?

XARA *gestures for them to go*. RUQAYA *joins her immediately.*

SABI. No. I mean, I've got comic club right after too, so...

RUQAYA. For real, Sabi, they got you studying harder in that club than for our *GCSEs*.

XARA. I don't bite.

SABI. It's not like that.

RUQAYA. Suit yourself.

XARA. Catch you another time, yeah?

RUQAYA *exits with* XARA. SABI *watches them for a moment, unhappy.*

SABI (*direct address*). Thing is, when they were saying we were these terrible people, like... dangerous. *Devious*. Plotting stuff with Xara, we weren't even *friends*. We'd fallen out. Big time. But Ruqaya carried on being her number-one fan.

Scene Three

A few days later. RUQAYA *is visiting* XARA*'s place for the first time.* XARA*'s bedroom is filled with books, photos, and there's a small desk that doubles for homework, make-up, and her influencer activist social-media empire.* RUQAYA *holds a small tripod.* XARA *is positioning a large sheet of cardboard covered in aluminium foil near the window.*

RUQAYA. Thought it would be bigger. Your stuff always looks so professional.

XARA. Awwww, you're so sweet. (*Of the tripod.*) Set that up there…

    RUQAYA *struggles with the tripod then sets up the phone.*

    Natural light's best but you have to catch the right time of day…

    XARA *checks her image in the phone, adjusts the foil-covered card.*

    Get a nice glow off this, see?

RUQAYA. Your mum is gorgeous, man. She must hit the gym *a lot*?

XARA. I don't live with my mum.

RUQAYA. Who's that downstairs, then?

XARA. My Aunt Sofia.

RUQAYA. Oh shit, sorry…

XARA. It's okay. Mum lives in Bangladesh. Got offered a job there, and my didima's really sick, so… [she went to help out]

RUQAYA. Oh right…

XARA. Want to see the edit of the one we did last week?

RUQAYA. I was just along for the ride, man…

XARA. You basically shot it.

RUQAYA. Just did what you told me to.

XARA. Okay, yeah, but you did good. Look.

XARA *plays her latest video for* RUQAYA. *Her onscreen persona is even more confident and charismatic than she is in real life.* RUQAYA *is completely star-struck.*

(*Onscreen.*) It's your girl Xara! Who *was* Fatima al-Fihriya and what does she have to do with libraries? (*Points to an image of Bibliotek.*) Well, let me tell you... Fatima El-Fihriya – (*Points to image offscreen.*) founded one of the oldest libraries in the world – (*Points to image offscreen.*) al-Qarawiyyin Library in Fez, Morocco. And get this – it's the oldest working library in the world. It is *still open* today. Housing over four thousand rare books and manuscripts, one of the most precious items in the collection is a hand-written copy of the Quran from the *ninth* century! So next time you come to 'Bibliotek', think of our sister Fatima and take inspiration from her love of learning. Right now, I'm an ambassador for a programme for people just like you, to come together to share our writing and our stories in a safe, supportive space. So if you want to join Safe Sisters – (*Points to image with logo offscreen.*) click the link below for info on how to sign up.

RUQAYA. You know I first met Sabi in the library?

XARA.... I did... not know that.

XARA *gets* RUQAYA *to sit on the chair near the window and checks the lighting on her phone.*

RUQAYA. My mum and her childminder took us to the same Rhyme Time session when we were bubbas. Only worked that out later though. There was a rainbow rug in the kids' corner with the alphabet and numbers and that's why I always see three as blue and A as red.

XARA. Oh, *interesting...*

RUQAYA. You know the librarians always thought we were sisters? Spent so much time together we were like family, yeah?

XARA. That's nice.

RUQAYA. Past tense, though.

XARA. Oh right…?

RUQAYA. She's so *distant* now, you know? Flaking out on me all the time. She doesn't even come *taco* night any more.

XARA. What do you think is going on with her…?

RUQAYA. You tell me, man.

XARA. I don't know. How would I know?

RUQAYA. Exactly. *Who* knows? The library's gone. My best friend's gone… Everything is off key, you know?

XARA. Listen, you don't have to sit around feeling sorry for yourself. You can come to Safe Sisters.

RUQAYA. You need bare peas to go in there now. It's not our library any more, it's 'Bibliotek'. In quotation marks. With a K.

XARA. Safe Sisters' workshops are *free*. That's the whole point. This is why they need ambassadors like me – to spread the word.

RUQAYA. For real?

XARA. Hundred per cent. Forget Sabi – her loss, right?

RUQAYA. Okay… Yeah… See, this is *why* you're an ambassador, man. So how did you get started at Safe Sisters?

XARA. It's a funny story, you know? I got into trouble one afternoon because my phone pinged in Spanish. Turned out it was a DM from Nadia…

Scene Four

RUQAYA *and* SABI *wait for the workshop to start in 'Bibliotek' café/workspace. This is the first time they've been here since it replaced their library.* SABI *takes a book down from one of the shelves.*

RUQAYA. *Tracy Beaker – classic.*

Of a pile of notebooks and pencils on one of the tables.

(*To* SABI.) Think these are free?

SABI. Looks like it.

RUQAYA (*taking a handful and pocketing them*). Nice.

XARA joins them. She wears a 'Safe Sisters' badge on her jacket.

SABI. Who was that?

XARA. Nadia – course leader.

SABI. Thought that was you?

RUQAYA (*tapping* XARA*'s badge*). She's an *ambassador*. (*Thick Spanish accent.*) Ms Maravilla.

She and XARA *laugh – an in-joke.* SABI *couldn't feel more excluded.*

(*To* SABI.) Sorry, oh no, sorry – she got a DM in Spanish, see? Oh it doesn't matter, you had to be there.

SABI (*of the book*). Can I take this out?

XARA. Haven't you read that one?

SABI. Yeah, but I'd like to read it again.

XARA. You can't take books home.

SABI. Why not?

XARA. You might not bring them back.

SABI. As a loan. I'm not going to steal it.

XARA. It's not like before, okay? You need to embrace the change.

SABI. I don't like change.

XARA. Surprised to see you here – doesn't it clash with comic club?

SABI. *No.* It's the only time Ruqs could hang out this weekend, so…

A knowing look between RUQAYA *and* XARA. XARA *starts the workshop.*

XARA. Okay. We're starting, everyone. Thank you. Thank you. Sit down. Yeah. There you go. Thank you so much for your patience, sisters. But as the saying goes, good things come to those who wait, right?

RUQAYA. Absolutely. I *always* say that.

SABI *rolls her eyes at* RUQAYA.

I do.

XARA. So I've been speaking to Nadia and we are *so* excited to see how much progress some of you have made over the past few sessions. Girls, it's *incredible*. It is *humbling* to see the difference Safe Sisters has already made to your lives. And you know, this is just the start, am I right?

RUQAYA *whoops.* SABI *is mortified.*

Plus it's good to see some new faces here today.

XARA *points to* RUQAYA *and* SABI.

The circle of sisters gets bigger and bigger. Now today's exercise is a bit more challenging. It's going to require a bit of digging, emotionally, but this is a safe space, remember? So anything you need to excavate or unravel or un*tie*, this is the place. Remember, our prompt for today's session was…

XARA *writes on the whiteboard on the wall.*

…'All about me.' And I've written something too, because everyone's equal here, never forget that. So let me warm things up for you by going first.

RUQAYA. Ms Maravilla, hit that piñata, yeah!

They both laugh. SABI*'s discomfited by yet another in joke.*

SABI. Are you talking about Ms. Marvel or something…?

RUQAYA. No, Sabi, don't worry.

SABI. Because I know you think it's for kids but if you just gave it a chance…

RUQAYA. It's not that deep, forget it.

XARA *takes a moment to prepare herself, then launches into her piece with confidence, spoken-word style.*

XARA. I am fury. I am rage. I am love. All on one page.
I am more than the skin I am in
But do you see me?
Because I see you.
I have no choice, or I have no voice
I must persuade you
Implore you
Beseech you
To look me in the eye
But I know this is too much to ask
So I will have to let it lie
And instead swallow all of your lies
About me.
So I am fury. I am rage. I am love. All on one page.

You could hear a pin drop. Even SABI *is quietly impressed.*

RUQAYA. Whoa.

XARA *just shrugs and sits back down.*

(*To* XARA.) You done that one before?

XARA. No, it's brand new.

SABI. Felt a bit rehearsed.

XARA. Don't have time to rehearse. I live in the moment. Speak how I feel.

RUQAYA. Yeah. Me too.

XARA (*to* RUQAYA). Come on then, let's hear what you've got?

RUQAYA. Yeah, alright.

RUQAYA stands up and clears her throat. She raps with forced confidence.

RUQAYA. I flow and I rhyme
    I got double time
    I swerve and I move
    I'm always foolproof
    I duck and I dive
    I'm free and I'm lithe
    So come say 'hiya'
    It's your girl, Ruqaya.

She ends with a flourish, maybe some hand signals.

XARA.…Great. So, what else have you got?

RUQAYA. Eh?

XARA. We're digging deep today, right? Speaking from the chest, speaking our *truth*. All I know from that is your name's Ruqaya.

SABI. It rhymed.

XARA. And you can rhyme.

RUQAYA. Okay… Alright then… I have something… Not sure if it's right, though?

XARA. There's no right or wrong here.

SABI. You told her she was wrong.

RUQAYA. I saw your video, the one about talking to your parents?

XARA. My TikTok on the importance of oral histories?

RUQAYA. That's the one, yeah.

XARA. Twenty-two thousand views and counting.

RUQAYA. It made me realise… how important *our* stories are…? Like, you don't have to be Shakespeare or whatever. You don't have to, you know, travel round the world on a yacht for people to want to hear what you have to say.

SABI. A yacht?

RUQAYA. You know what I mean, yeah? You don't need shiny shoes, or or, a Rolex.

SABI. A Rolex?

RUQAYA. Will you let me finish, Sabi?

SABI. Sorry.

RUQAYA. I spoke to my mum. Like, really spoke to her. And you know, it made me feel… rich? Get what I mean? Made me feel like we have… *history*… Or something, I dunno…

She doubts herself. Looks to XARA *for reassurance.*

XARA. What did you talk about?

RUQAYA. I asked her what it was like when she was my age. Like, who was her favourite teacher? What did she like doing after school? What sort of music did she like? And I swear, once she got started, she couldn't stop. She told me how she used to write stories. And one of her stories got in the local paper, because she came second in a national writing competition. Second place! It was about her pet, this budgie. A budgerigar. People used to keep them. They came in different colours and stuff. Hers was blue. I know it seems a bit off now, keeping a bird in a cage, but this was years ago. And she loved her budgie. She called it Farouk, because she always wanted a little brother called Farouk, but she had two sisters instead. I can tell you a bit of the story if you like?

She looks around for support. SABI *nods,* XARA *whoops.*

XARA. Go for it!

RUQAYA. Okay, sick. So… Mum wrote about how Farouk looked out of the window and looked at the television, as if they were the same thing. She wasn't sure if he knew the difference. Did he think Cilla Black was part of our family? She was a TV presenter on this show. Or did he think my mum was on primetime? Farouk sang along to the theme tune of *Newsround*, and the *Six O'Clock News*. Farouk sang along when *Neighbours* started. Farouk sang so sweetly. Mum wondered if he'd sing as sweetly outside? Would it sound even better? Or would his song be drowned out by all the other birds? She thought: 'Maybe in here he's special? Because in here he's one of a kind. Farouk. Our Farouk.'

Silence.

Yeah?

XARA *claps and cheers.*

XARA. Hell yeah! Amazing level of *detail*.

RUQAYAH. Mr Pietrowski says you can learn anything off by heart if it *speaks* to your heart. Used to have him for English. But now I'm in Mrs Montague's class.

XARA. Give it up everyone for our sister Ruqaya. *Smashing* it.

XARA *holds up her hand for a high-five.* RUQAYA *jubilantly responds, overcome with emotion.*

(*To* SABI.) Okay, now it's your turn.

SABI. I'm alright, thanks.

XARA. We'd love to hear from you.

SABI. Nah, it's okay.

RUQAYA. You have to read, Sabi.

SABI. No I don't.

XARA. Come on. I'll tell you what, I'll record you? If it's good enough maybe I'll use it in one of my videos?

XARA *takes out her phone and starts to record* SABI. *This only makes* SABI *clam up more.*

RUQAYA. *Sick*. Come on, Sabi.

SABI. I'm not reading something out loud to a bunch of strangers.

RUQAYA. Just pretend we're not here.

SABI (*to* XARA). Can you please get that out of my face?

XARA. Your voice matters. You know that?

SABI. Maybe try listening to me then?

RUQAYA. You think too much, Sabi, that's your problem.

SABI. How can you *think* too much? (*To* XARA.) Stop it, can you just stop it?

SABI *pushes the phone away, gets up and exits.*

RUQAYA. Sabi?

XARA. She always like that?

RUQAYA. Yeah, pretty much. You've either got it or you haven't, you know?

Scene Five

XARA *has her usual session debrief with* NADIA *in Nadia's office.*

NADIA. Farouk? It's a really lovely piece of writing – I'll put it in Ruqaya's file.

XARA *gives her* RUQAYA's *work.*

I'll also need the phone back.

XARA.…What's that?

NADIA. You were aware of the guidelines about usage when we allocated it to you. You signed the form.

XARA. Nadia... You can't... *take my phone*.

NADIA. It's Safe Sisters' property.

XARA. You know mine is bust, though?

NADIA. This is a red line for us – I'm sorry.

XARA. I did it for *Sabi*. I was trying to get her to loosen up.

NADIA. Then it backfired.

XARA....You asked *me* to be an ambassador. You practically begged me to come on board.

NADIA. And we need our ambassadors to set an example.

XARA. But it's got all my videos on it...

NADIA. They must be on the cloud, surely?

XARA. Right, but how can I access them when *my phone is bust*?!

NADIA. This is something you're going to have to work out on your own, Xara.

XARA. You wanted my clout but you didn't want my voice. Got it.

XARA *hands over her phone, her hand shaking. She is immediately bereft.*

Scene Six

RUQAYA *and* SABI *wait outside 'Bibliotek'.*

SABI (*direct address*). And maybe if we'd just gone straight home none of it would have happened. But no, Ruqs made sure we were still hanging round outside 'Bibliotek'. Cursed place.

RUQAYA (*direct address*). With a K.

SABI (*to* RUQAYA). Did she even ask you to wait for her?

RUQAYA. Just give her a chance, Sabi. Sound jealous or something.

SABI. Shut up.

RUQAYA. You're always at comic club anyways. What's the problem?

SABI *grows silent.*

SABI. Ruqs, it's time I told you something. I mean… I've been trying to tell you something for *time* now….

RUQAYA. For real, Sabi, your eye *again*. What is up with that?

SABI*'s eye is twitching.* XARA *enters, brimming with rage, grabbing* RUQAYA*'s attention immediately.*

XARA (*to* RUQAYA). Can I borrow your phone?

SABI (*under her breath*). *Seriously?*

RUQAYA. Yeah, course… Why?

She gives XARA *her phone.*

XARA. Because we're here to *protest.*

RUQAYA. Sick.

SABI. Against what?

XARA. How about a *violation* of my human rights?

SABI. Really?

XARA. I'm talking the theft of my freedom of expression, my freedom of *thought*, *and* my *intellectual property.*

SABI. What happened in there?

XARA. Get this. (*To* RUQAYA.) Are you getting this?

RUQAYA. I'm getting it.

XARA. Let's go live.

RUQAYA *starts recording* XARA.

That… *woman* just *took my phone*.

RUQAYA. What? She can't do that.

SABI. I thought she'd *hit* you or something.

XARA. She hit me alright – she hit me with *injustice*.

RUQAYA. That is not on.

XARA. She hit me with *censorship*. She hit me with *repression*. What she doesn't understand is I've got a right to hit back, and you better believe I will.

RUQAYA. What're you going to do?

XARA. Expose them, of course.

SABI. Expose who?

XARA. Safe Sisters. Writing workshops here at 'Bibliotek'. It's not even a real library. You can't take books out.

SABI. Yeah, that's what I said.

XARA (*of* SABI). My sister here wanted to read *Tracy Beaker* – could she borrow a copy?

RUQAYA *turns her phone towards* SABI.

SABI. Don't drag me into this?

XARA. Too late, girl, you started it.

SABI. How'd you work that one out?

XARA. I was trying to *empower* you, and they turn around and do *this*? (*To the phone camera.*) These poor girls used to rely on this place. It was a home from home. Place to shelter from the rain. Place to hide from racist, Islamophobic bullies.

RUQAYA. It's true, man. We were robbed. Simple as that.

SABI. It's not that deep? We just moved onto Coffee Republic.

RUQAYA. Coffee Republic does not have *Tracy Beaker*, Sabi.

XARA. That's right. (*Straight to camera*.) All they've got at
Safe Sisters is fake smiles, fake words and fake *books*.

RUQAYA *starts to spontaneously start rapping*.

RUQAYA (*starts to rap*). Fake books, fake books
Think you're so clever,
Fake books, fake books
Think you're so wise
Fake books, fake books,
You think that we'll never…
Fake books, fake books
Open our *eyes*.

RUQAYA *repeats this chorus several times under* XARA*'s
spoken word/rant*.

XARA. Listen up, boycott Safe Sisters' writing workshops.
Boycott 'Bibliotek'. I'm telling you this place is more like
Unsafe Sisters, the way they violate young people's human
rights. The way they talk down to you. The way they make
you feel small. But I'm telling you, I stand tall in my truth
and I stand on the shoulders of *giants* so you better believe
I'm not about to be pushed around or taken advantage of
and if they don't give me my phone back there is going to be
trouble. They're Jim Crow and I'm Rosa Parks. You get me?
They're the East India Company and I'm Gandhi. I'm Begum
Hazrat Mahal and they're the *British Army*. So they better
watch it, yeah? Because there are going to be *consequences*.

RUQAYA. Dry Safe Sisters, trying to make us small
Next to you, wastemen, I'm ten foot tall
Their squash is warm, their snacks are haram
They're pretending to care but they don't give a… damn

RUQAYA *and* XARA. Fake books, fake books
Think you're so clever,
Fake books, fake books
Think you're so wise
Fake books, fake books,
You think that we'll never…
Fake books, fake books
Open our *eyes*.

RUQAYA (*direct address*). And that's when Nadia arrived. Did she feel her ears burning or something?

SABI *becomes* NADIA.

NADIA. Stop recording right now – I'm warning you.

RUQAYA (*direct address*). Xara blew up. If it was a cartoon, there'd be steam blowing out of her ears. Or, or, it was like when Neo first meets Agent Smith.

XARA. You can't tell me what to do.

NADIA. I'm starting to think you weren't a good fit for Safe Sisters anyway.

XARA. Yeah, well, I don't think that *blouse* is a good fit.

RUQAYA (*direct address*). Xara took a biscuit from her pocket – she must have stashed it at the workshop. And she threw it right at Nadia – for real, you should have seen it.

NADIA. Nooooo youuuuuuu doooooooooon't…

RUQAYA (*direct address*). She was lucky that time – it sailed past her right ear and exploded in crumbs on the pavement.

XARA. You don't get to tell me what to do any more, waste sister!

RUQAYA (*direct address*). If you think Nadia rose above this, you'd be wrong. She took a Funsize Twix from her handbag and chucked it at Xara at *full speed*. Xara went full *Matrix* and dodged that tasty treat like Trinity herself. She pulled out another biscuit – this time a custard cream. Where did she get it from? Was it literally up her sleeve? Nadia couldn't believe it – she didn't stand a chance. Xara threw it full force and it hit Nadia right between the eyes…

XARA. What's the matter? Out of ammo?

RUQAYA (*direct address*). Nadia wasn't done yet, though. She goes up to Xara and pulls the Safe Sisters badge off her top. *Un*ceremonious.

NADIA. You're not fit to wear this.

XARA. Yeah, well, I quit.

NADIA. You can't quit if you're fired.

NADIA *exits in fury.*

Scene Seven

RUQAYA *and* SABI *are with* XARA *in Xara's bedroom.*

SABI. What's the big emergency? Why did you call us round?

XARA. They came and got me out of physics at ten thirty a.m.

She draws a line showing the route from the physics classroom to the head's office.

They took me the long way round. Probably to psych me out. They didn't even tell me where we were going. And I was thinking, am I behind on any of my homework? I mean, I cut it a bit fine with my Spanish but I still got it in at the start of the lesson, por la piel de mis dientes. Maybe Auntie Sofia forgot to top up my lanyard for lunch? She's done that a couple of times now... I was thinking, 'I could call her and ask, if I *had a phone.*' If I rang from the office would she even pick up? She wouldn't recognise the number... Bun Nadia, man! We'd got all the way to C Block by the time I realised we were heading to Sanderson's office. I was like, whoa, the *head*, must be serious. But he wasn't there.

SABI. So who was?

RUQAYA. One of the deputies? Mrs Peters?

XARA. No.

RUQAYA. Ooh, I know, Mrs Santos.

SABI. Why would it be Mrs Santos?

RUQAYA. She said it could be her Spanish homework?

XARA. Guys, it was nothing to do with my Spanish homework.
There wasn't even a teacher there. Just a woman from the
council and this cop.

SABI. The cops were there...? What did they want?

XARA. I don't know.

RUQAYA. What the hell is going on?

SABI. What did they say?

XARA. They asked me all these questions. Did I go mosque?
Which mosque? Did I pray five times a day? Does my mum
pray five times a day? Do we fast at Ramadan? What do I
think about Muslims who don't? Where's my dad? Does *he*
go mosque?

RUQAYA. What did you say?

XARA. I told him that would be tricky seeing as he's dead.

RUQAYA....Oh...

SABI....Shit, Xara. I'm sorry.

XARA. I stopped answering when they asked how he died.
They know all about that at school. What're they bothering
me for? Then they played the video we made....

SABI. Hold up... What video?

XARA. The one we did outside 'Bibliotek'. Fake Books.

SABI. The video *you* made, you mean?

RUQAYA. We were there too, Sabi.

XARA. They wanted to know what I meant about Gandhi, and
Rosa Parks and Begum Hazrat Mahal – although you know
I don't think they knew who she was? They kept asking if I
meant Shamima Begum? And I was like, if I meant Shamima
Begum I would have said Shamima Begum, wouldn't I?

SABI. What did they want to know?

XARA. Like... How did I know about these people? I wanted to
say there's been a *Horrible Histories* about Rosa Parks, what

are you, dumb? But like I said I was keeping my mouth shut.
Until I had my lawyer present.

RUQAYA. You have a lawyer?

XARA. No, that's the problem, see? And they just said 'Oh so
you're not going to cooperate then?'

SABI. Who put them onto you?

XARA. …I don't know. But think I've narrowed it down…

She uses the whiteboard to illustrate her theories.

Suspect one: Mr Pietrowski.

RUQAYA. What? Shut up, he wouldn't do that.

XARA. He's the one who pulled me out of Physics. You
should've seen him – bare serious, steely jawed. Wouldn't
even *look* at me. Made me feel like some cheap-ass criminal.
And all he could say when I asked him what was going on
was 'You'll find out soon enough'.

RUQAYA. Mr Pietrowski's not like that. Must have been having
an off day.

SABI. Maybe it wasn't his idea. Maybe he was just doing what
he was told.

XARA. Yeah. Could be trying to impress Sanderson. Who's
bare old. Probably looking to retire. Maybe Pietrowski likes
the look of that headteacher's office? Sees himself in that
pleather chair.

RUQAYA. He'd be a *great* head.

XARA. Motive – see? That's what I'm talking about. Which
brings me to suspect two: Steph.

Stunned silence.

SABI. …Could she do that?

XARA. I don't know… Maybe. Probably.

SABI. Can't be right.

XARA. She's pissed at me for sticking up for you two losers. She's trying to get her own back like the petty little bitch she is. If it is her, this is your fault.

SABI. Er, no, I don't think so.

XARA. Suspect three: Nadia.

RUQAYA. Yeah, you're right – she's really sus.

SABI. She wouldn't do that.

XARA. She took my phone, didn't she?

SABI. She's one of us.

XARA. She's intimidated by me – my talent, my courage, my *spark*.

SABI *stifles laughter.*

SABI. If you say so.

XARA. She looks at me and she sees her younger self.

RUQAYA. Her eyeliner is a bit like yours.

XARA. She's resentful. She'll do anything to cut me down.

RUQAYA.…Who was your Begum woman again?

SABI. Shamima?

XARA. *No. Begum Hazrat Mahal.* Don't you know anything? I did a video all about her? Didn't you see it? Last July.

RUQAYA. Ah, that was the summer I dropped my phone down the toilet. (*To* SABI.) Remember? Tried the rice trick but it didn't work.

XARA. She helped drive the British out of India. But she was up for more of a fight than Gandhi.

RUQAYA *and* SABI *are both struggling to take this all in.*

You know? When they stole all their land? And starved them? And hung loads of them? Made them work for next to nothing. Raped and killed loads of them? You know?

RUQAYA....Oh.

Beat. RUQAYA *and* SABI *are now quite frightened.*

SABI. Why did you say that?

XARA. Why not?

SABI *(to* RUQAYA). I didn't even want to wait for her.
I wanted to go home.

XARA. I was making a point, wasn't I? About standing up to
oppression. (*To* RUQAYA.) And anyway, it was on *your*
phone. And you're the one who tagged Safe Sisters.

SABI. *Ruqaya...*

RUQAYA *is very much in over her head.*

XARA. She tagged the council. She tagged the *prime minister.*
Total rockstar behaviour, to be honest.

RUQAYA. Might have got a bit carried away...

XARA. They asked me how long I'd been into politics.

SABI. How long *have* you been into politics?

XARA. Take an interest in what they don't teach us at school.
What's wrong with that?

SABI. *You* said it, and you made the video. The cops are on
to *you* because of your... instagram or whatever. It's got
nothing to do with us and we're not getting involved.

RUQAYA. That is cold, Sabi.

SABI. This isn't our problem.

XARA. What're you worried about? Your precious boater?

SABI. Shut up.

RUQAYA. Boating?

XARA. Sabi's going St Saviour's.

SABI *(to* XARA). I hate you.

RUQAYA. Yeah, right. St Saviour's – good one. With those stuck-up clowns.

RUQAYA *starts to laugh, assuming* XARA*'s joking, then sees* SABI*'s face.*

SABI (*to* RUQAYA). I have been trying to tell you... a *million* times...

RUQAYA. We're going Everyman. Together. We've got the route all worked out – no more Stop BE. No more umbrellas. Bubble Tea every Friday. They let you go *off site* for lunch...

SABI. ...I didn't think I'd get in.

RUQAYA *is aghast.*

RUQAYA. ...You been lying to me?

SABI (*of* XARA). She was at the exam as well.

RUQAYA*'s overwhelmed by all this.*

XARA. I'm not going St Saviour's. I'll be at Everyman College with you.

SABI. Oh wow, you flunked it? Thought you were a genius or something?

XARA. As if. Have fun with all your Karens.

RUQAYA. You've *both* been lying...?

RUQAYA *grabs her bag.*

SABI. I didn't mean to, Ruqs...

RUQAYA *exits, heartbroken.*

XARA. Where're you going? Ruqaya?

SABI *hurries after her.*

(*Calling after them.*) I'm better off without you losers anyway. Talk about dead weight, yeah?

She sits on the floor, alone, the silence increasingly unbearable.

Scene Eight

XARA *unravels, isolated and lacking focus and connection without her phone. She tries to write a script for a new video.*

XARA. It's your girl Xara… Who is Xara Hussein? Who *is* Xara Hussein…? …Who *was* Xara Hussein?

RUQAYA sits alone in her bedroom. She receives a notification on her phone. Then another.

Then another. Her phone rings.

RUQAYA. (*picking up*) Hello…?

She hangs up, scared. Notification after notification pings on her phone. She silences it. It buzzes, ringing again. She throws it on the floor. It buzzes so hard it moves across the floor by itself, like a living, nefarious monster. RUQAYA *edges as far away from it as possible.*

SABI'*s alone in her bedroom, trying on her new school uniform for the grammar school, including the notorious boater. She looks at herself in the mirror, then takes off the hat, frustrated, flinging it onto the floor. She rallies, puts on some music and practises one of her and Ruqaya's old dance routines, diligent and focused. She gets some of the steps wrong, stops the music and starts again from the top. This happens a couple of times. She grows increasingly frustrated and turns off the music. A moment of isolation and upset.*

The distance between the girls grows bigger and bigger, as the space they each inhabit diminishes. They get smaller too.

Scene Nine

A few days later. SABI *enters and finds* RUQAYA *lying down on the street outside 'Bibliotek'.*

SABI (*direct address*). Next time I saw Ruqaya she was lying on the pavement outside 'Bibliotek'. Did *not* look good… (*To* RUQAYA.) What are you doing?

RUQAYA. Giving up.

SABI. How long have you been here?

RUQAYA. Dunno.

SABI. Your mum's worried about you. We've been looking everywhere. Why haven't you been answering your phone?

RUQAYA. It's at home.

SABI. You forgot it?

RUQAYA. No.

Confused beat.

SABI. Ruqaya, what the hell, man? It's not even eight o'clock.

RUQAYA. Couldn't sleep.

SABI (*touching her shoulder*). Aren't you getting cold?

RUQAYA. No.

SABI. Why're you sticky?

RUQAYA. Steph and that lot came past. One of them had a can of Fanta.

SABI. Oh no, Ruqs…

RUQAYA. I don't care.

SABI. Come on, let's get to school – we're going be late.

RUQAYA (*game-show-buzzer sound*). U-errrrr. Negative.

SABI. You have to move before they open.

RUQAYA. Why?

SABI. You're in the way of the door.

RUQAYA. They can step over me.

SABI. But... you'll get into trouble.

RUQAYA. Too late.

SABI. Why? What's happened?

Beat.

RUQAYA. They kept ringing and ringing, texts every hour. I tried to ignore it at first but eventually it just seemed easier to do what they said.

SABI. What who said?

RUQAYA. This woman at the council. Said she was the Prevent Officer or something.

SABI. Prevent Officer?

RUQAYA. She wanted to look at my social media and stuff.

SABI. About that video again? Fake Books? Just tell them it was all Xara.

RUQAYA. No. I don't know. She was asking me all these questions.

SABI. ...Did she say anything about me?

RUQAYA. Why would she?

SABI. Just want to know if I'm getting called in next.

RUQAYA. You are something else, you know? It's not all about you.

SABI. ...I didn't mean it like that. I just meant... I don't think they're even allowed to do that.

RUQAYA. You don't know anything, Sabi. It doesn't make any sense. It's not natural, it doesn't rhyme, it's *off key*.

SABI. Have you told your mum?

RUQAYA. She's pissed at me. Says she doesn't have time for all this and no one in our family's been in trouble with the cops before and I'm not allowed on my phone. Just hit two thousand followers on the IG as well.

SABI. So is this like a protest or something? Like a one-girl action?

RUQAYA. I'm not a one-girl action any more. What would be the point?

SABI. ...So you're giving up? Like, properly?

RUQAYA. Should never have trusted you. Either of you.

SABI. Don't say that.

RUQAYA. You telling me what I'm allowed to say now?

SABI. You can say whatever you like to me, you know that.

RUQAYA. How about this, then? Fuck off.

Beat, then SABI *sits down beside her.* RUQAYA *kicks her, hard.*

SABI. Ow.

RUQAYA. Just leave me *alone*.

SABI. I'm not leaving you here by yourself.

RUQAYA. You're a liar and she's a phoney.

SABI *carefully takes a seat a bit further away.*

SABI. You know I've been walking around trying to work out when to tell you… It's pretty much all I've thought about for weeks now… The only reason I want to go St Saviour's is because you can do Astronomy for A level there. And the only reason I like Astronomy is because we used to look at the sky on the way home from school when it was getting dark and you were the first person who ever told me about the pole star. How it's the brightest, the first one you can see at night. And that was what made me want to find out about all the others as well. You're my pole star, Ruqs.

Beat. RUQAYA *considers this for a moment, then kicks her again.*

Oyah. Stop it.

RUQAYA. You are a *betrayer*. You're pissing off to St Saviour's without me because you *want* to. Stop making excuses. Just… go *away*.

RUQAYA *bends her legs and then releases them in a kick, pushing* SABI *as far away from her as she can without moving from her spot.* SABI *almost falls over. She reluctantly gets up.*

SABI. Okay fine. I can see you need your space. (*Direct address*.) And I knew I had to do something, it was obvious. But I didn't really know what.

SABI *reluctantly exits.*

Scene Ten

SABI *psychs herself up to finally read. She's clearly rehearsed it several times.*

SABI (*direct address*). I went to stop BE, as usual, except I was by myself. And I could see Steph and that lot getting on. The next bus wasn't for twenty minutes though, and I didn't want to get a detention for being late, so I decided to just… go for it. I tell myself this is like Moon Girl, the first time she goes up against Kid Kree. I could do this…

SABI *flounders, self-conscious in front of all of those in attendance, struggling with the trauma of this memory.* RUQAYA *starts to beatbox.* SABI *looks over at her.* RUQAYA *offers a supportive thumbs up.* SABI *smiles, touched. She continues, with* RUQAYA*'s support.*

I almost sat downstairs, behind the driver, kept my head down. But I was thinking of *Ms. Marvel*, *issue thirty-four*, where Kamala Khan learns she embiggens by drawing on the strength of all her future and past selves. And I imagined myself in five years, graduating from uni. And getting my first job. And maybe some time in the future, finding a new star, and deciding what to name it. And naming it after my daughter, or my son. And I took all the power and the courage from all the past and future Sabis and I *did* feel bigger. So I headed upstairs. All the way to the back. And part of me was thinking, Ms. Marvel doesn't have a death wish though, does she? But maybe I did, because I sat down right across the aisle from them. They were laughing at me and saying stuff but I just got my phone out, and googled 'Prevent Officer checking phone – allowed?' And I found this bare long document, really official-looking. I skimmed the first page or two but that was enough. 'Our counter-terrorism strategy contains a plan to prevent radicalisation and stop would-be terrorists from committing mass murder. Osama Bin Laden may be dead, but the threat from Al Qaeda inspired terrorism is not.' And my heart must have stopped and it sort of felt like the whole world had stopped, you know? All I could see were those words. 'Terrorists.' 'Mass murder.' Is this why Nadia took Xara's phone? Is this why Mr Pietrowski pulled her out of Physics? Is this why someone at the council wanted to see Ruqaya's social media? Is this what they think of us…? But before I could have a proper read, Steph got up and stood over me, and she was laughing so hard and she looked so proud of herself, and she said 'Who do you think you are, Rosa Parks? Move.' And I looked at her, and all I could think about was Ruqs, and her coat, and how sticky it was. And Xara and how she you know, *lives* on her phone? And it just sort of… came out of my mouth. 'No, I won't.' And she said 'Thought they would've deported you by now.' And I realised I was nothing like Moon Girl or Ms. Marvel, and Steph was nothing like Kid Kree. This was real life and I couldn't let Steph or anyone else hold me back. So I just stayed put and kept on reading. And eventually she got bored and went back to her friends and they were laughing about me all the way and shouting 'Oi, Shamima' every now and then but I barely heard them to be honest. We got to the stop outside school and they all got off, but I decided to keep on going. I had to go to Safe Sisters. I had to speak to Nadia.

XARA *recounts her mission at the same time and the two accounts now interweave, like dual protagonists in a split-screen comic strip.*

XARA (*direct address*). Around the same time I took three buses to the nearest actual library. As usual it was up to me to sort everything out because as usual no one else gave a shit, so I was on my own. I needed to do some digging.

SABI (*direct address*). I hung around by the fake books for a while, pretending to browse, but I was getting worried. What if Nadia wasn't in today? How long should I wait?

XARA (*direct address*). I swiped a notebook from Aunt Sofia and I took my pencil case – old school. The man on the desk showed me how to find the government stuff in the reference section. Here's what I found. The UK's Prevent strategy was introduced in 2003. It's supposed to 'stop people becoming terrorists' by referring people to the police. Mostly for things they've said, watched, written or read. It's not for people who've actually broken the law. Everyone who works in the public sector is supposed to look out for signs that people might become terrorists.

SABI (*direct address*). I'll be honest, I wanted to leave, more than anything, but I made myself stay there.

XARA (*direct address*). Some of the things they look out for in people are: feelings of grievance and injustice; a feeling of being under threat, a need for identity, meaning and belonging...

SABI (*direct address*). I did all the exercises my mum taught me. To ground myself. Five things I could see. A floor lamp. A bin. A banana peel in the bin. A pigeon outside the window. Pigeon shit.

XARA (*direct address*). A desire for excitement and adventure, a desire for political or moral change, being at a transitional time of life…

SABI (*direct address*). Four things I could touch. The worry beads in my pocket. My keys in my other pocket. The carpet beneath my feet. The loose thread inside my left sock when I scrunched my toes.

XARA (*direct address*). A vocal or active opposition to our fundamental British values, overidentification with a group, cause or ideology, attempting to recruit others to that group, cause or ideology…

SABI (*direct address*). Three things I could hear. A fan whirring. Someone typing on their laptop. The traffic outside.

XARA (*direct address*). Being aggrieved about domestic policies and/or international affairs, using extremist narratives and a global ideology to explain personal disadvantage, a misconception and/or rejection of UK foreign policy…

SABI (*direct address*). Two things I could smell. The banana skin. Someone chewing minty gum.

XARA (*direct address*). A distrust of Western media reporting, becoming increasingly angry about issues or events they feel are unfair or unjust, adopting an us versus them worldview…

SABI (*direct address*). One thing I could taste. Fear. It's sort of metallic? Like sucking on your spoon too long after the yoghurt's gone. Or that pink stuff they give you at the dentist to swill around your mouth after you've had a filling. I have a lot of fillings…

XARA (*direct address*). Single-issue ideologies that rely on narratives that seek to change a specific policy or practice, for example animal rights, anti-abortion, anti-fascism.

XARA *and* SABI *briefly touch hands as they cross, as their mission becomes a shared one…*

SABI (*direct address*). I could taste my fillings as Nadia walked over, in a hurry, red lipstick, killer heels. It's impressive how fast she was going on those things, for real.

Scene Eleven

SABI *and* NADIA *are in* NADIA*'s office*.

NADIA. I hope you haven't quit the sessions because of Xara?

SABI. I only came to Safe Sisters because of *Ruqaya*.

NADIA. Well, tell Xara she can come in any time to get her phone.

SABI. I don't see her much any more.

NADIA. So why are you here?

SABI. I need your help. Why are the police hassling Xara? Why do the council want Ruqaya's phone? What's going on?

NADIA. The police? What's happened?

SABI. You tell me.

NADIA. How would I know?

SABI. Is this something to do with Prevent?

NADIA. …Why would you say that?

SABI. Something the woman at the council said to Ruqaya. And I've been reading up on it and I was wondering if it's that. *Is it* that?

NADIA. You think Ruqaya's been referred to Channel?

SABI. Which Channel?

NADIA. That's what it's called.

SABI. No one's told us anything.

NADIA. They refer you to Channel if... they think you need extra support.

SABI. Doesn't feel like support. Feels like someone's snitched on us.

NADIA. I don't think you should view it like... snitching.

SABI. How should I view it?

NADIA. It's supposed to be an early intervention.

SABI. To what?

NADIA. To help people at a... vulnerable age.

SABI. You think Ruqaya's vulnerable?

NADIA. No. I mean... I don't know her well enough to say.

SABI. Could Steph and that lot have done this?

NADIA. Who?

SABI. These girls who pick on us at school.

NADIA. I don't know... Possibly.

SABI. Mr Pietrowski?

NADIA. Teachers can refer students if they have concerns.

SABI. It was him then?

NADIA. I couldn't say.

SABI. Was it you?

NADIA. I wouldn't do that.

SABI. I thought you said it was a good thing? 'Early intervention'?

NADIA. It was my idea to bring in ambassadors, you know?

SABI. We just wanted to write poetry. I mean, Ruqaya did. I'm more into comics. *Graphic novels*.

NADIA. Well, that's exactly what the sessions are for. I wanted girls like you to be *empowered*, to find your voice.

SABI. I've got a voice.

NADIA. There's no funding for projects like this. We had to beg steal and borrow to make Safe Sisters happen. I saw the video Ruqaya uploaded. She tagged our funders. She tagged the *prime minister*.

SABI. Funders? Who are they?

NADIA. ...It's all on our website.

SABI. Was it them?

NADIA. I didn't say that.

SABI. What are you saying, exactly?

NADIA. There's nothing else like this in the area, you know? You're probably too young to remember this but we used to have youth clubs round here. Sports clubs. I'm just trying to create space for young people like you. People can give funding, but they can also take it away. It's not just about you. We're talking about the whole project here.

SABI (*direct address*). I realised I wasn't getting *any* answers from Nadia. But I noticed the window was open. And I could smell vanilla.

Scene Twelve

SABI *and* RUQAYA *and* XARA *are in Xara's bedroom the next day.*

SABI. She swears it wasn't her.

RUQAYA. People lie though, don't they, Sabi?

SABI *can't answer.*

XARA. Someone else at Safe Sisters, then? Or someone at the council?

RUQAYA. Maybe it was Rishi Sunak?

XARA. It just takes one person to 'raise concerns'.

RUQAYA. Concerns about what?

SABI. Like, not about a crime, but something, before a crime...
Like, before you've committed a crime. Or thought about
committing a crime.

XARA. Like a pre-crime?

RUQAYA. I'm like a pre-criminal?

SABI. You're not a criminal, Ruqs.

RUQAYA. Why's everyone making me feel like one, then?
Walked into the common room this afternoon and everyone
stopped talking and just... looked at me.

SABI. It's in your head.

RUQAYA. Walked past Mr Pietrowski after History this
morning and he blanked me.

SABI. ...Probably didn't see you.

RUQAYA. He *always* says hello. Asks what I'm reading.
They've got to him too. Mr Pietrowski. Oh my days...?
What if it was him? It's a pre-crime, man, it's a pre-crime,
it's a pre-crime...

XARA (*to* SABI). What I don't understand is why you didn't
get my phone back.

SABI. We're going to.

RUQAYA. No way I'm going Safe Sisters. Never again.

SABI. Not for a session. I know how to get in after hours.
Look...

She draws up a plan on the whiteboard.

This is the front entrance, right? Looking out to the square.
There's that big window here, on the left, and there's the
alleyway down the side. And there are three CCTV cameras
on the street outside, here, here, and here.

XARA. How do you know?

SABI. It's called paying attention. To the little things. There's a window at the back, high up. I reckon she always keeps it open because she vapes in there.

XARA. I've never seen her vaping.

SABI. One fell out of her pocket when you two were arguing. Vanilla flavour.

XARA. So… you just want to break in?

SABI. We don't know what they've said about us. We don't know what info they have on us. We don't know what it means for us in the future… It's the opposite of *Ms. Marvel issue thirty-four*.

XARA. What?

RUQAYA. The one where she finds out how she embiggens. (*To* SABI.) You left your copy in my room.

SABI. And you read it?

A moment of connection between them.

Think about it. Going on holiday and waiting in the queue for passport control. What does it say about you on the screen? You get smaller. Going to a protest, like when the library was getting shut down. Wondering what the police already know about you. Wondering if they're watching you. You get smaller. Applying for your first job at Greenwich Observatory…

RUQAYA (*to* XARA). It's her dream role.

SABI. Wondering if your CV's been flagged. Wondering what it says about you on file. Wondering if you *have* a file. I don't want to get smaller and smaller. That's not how it's supposed to work. And we're not breaking anything. We're just… taking back what's ours. Xara's videos on her phone, *our* stories.

RUQAYA. Farouk?

SABI. Definitely Farouk.

RUQAYA (*to* SABI). But what if we get caught?

SABI….I'll say it was my idea.

RUQAYA. They'll kick you out of St Saviour's before you've even started.

SABI. If they do, then… I don't want to go there.

XARA (*direct address*). I finally broke the news to my mum. Thought maybe she could help, you know? She put together a subject access request for the council with my Auntie Sofia. It's an official way of getting any organisation to send you the files they have on record about you. Mum said they had to respond, legally. She was like – that's *your* data. This is what they sent back.

She holds up a sheet of A4, the text of which has almost entirely been blacked out.

(*Direct address.*) Jokes, right? There's about, five words you can actually read.

RUQAYA (*direct address*). Tell them what it says if you read it diagonally.

XARA (*direct address*). No, we talked about this.

RUQAYA (*direct address*). 'Everyman likes front bottom.' You know like front bottom…

She *points but is laughing too hard to finish.* SABI *and* XARA *exchange a weary look.*

SABI (*direct address*). We never found out who referred us.

XARA (*direct address*). We never found out what we were referred *for.*

SABI (*direct address*). We didn't have any choice, see? We had to take matters into our *own* hands.

XARA (*direct address*). But we were finally united.

SABI (*direct address*). And we realised we had to tell everyone else what was going on.

RUQAYA (*direct address*). About pre-crimes. So there was only one thing for it…

They start to dance in formation.

(*Rapping.*) It's a pre-crime
For something you might be thinking of further down the line
It's a pre-crime
For something you might decide to do at a future point in time
It's a pre-crime
No sweat you bet it's fine if you'll just change your mind
If not, it's a pre-crime, it's a pre-crime, it's a pre-crime.

XARA. Say they're preventing us from criming
When all we want to do is rhyming

ALL. It's a pre-crime
For something you might be thinking of further down the line
It's a pre-crime
For something you might decide to do at a future point in time
It's a pre-crime
No sweat you bet it's fine if you'll just change your mind
If not it's a pre-crime, it's a pre-crime, it's a pre-criiiiiiiiiiime.

They finish with a flourish.

XARA (*direct address*). This is why what happened, happened.

RUQAYA (*direct address*). This is why we did what we did.

SABI (*direct address*). They didn't leave us with any other choice. We had to take the fight to *them*.

XARA (*direct address*). 'Bibliotek'.

SABI (*direct address*). In quotation marks.

RUQAYA (*direct address*). With a K.

Scene Thirteen

Darkness. A few days later after sundown. XARA *waits in the square outside 'Bibliotek', self-conscious, nervous. She paces, then realises she's pacing, and stops herself.* RUQAYA *and* SABI *enter and join her, also in sweatshirts with the hoods pulled down over their faces.* RUQAYA *has a fold-up step ladder.* XARA *hands out high-viz tabards and torches from her rucksack. They put them on and switch on their torches.*

SABI (*direct address*). Thursday eleventh of April 2024. The first ever action from a mysterious new group.

RUQAYA (*direct address*). We still need a name.

SABI (*direct address*). Yeah, I know.

RUQAYA (*direct address*). How about WAP?

XARA (*direct address*). What? *No.*

RUQAYA (*direct address*). Women Against Prevent.

XARA *and* SABI *are unimpressed.*

XARA (*direct address*). An *anonymous* new group. Three ordinary girls, with nothing in common. Except the one thing that mattered. A burning desire for justice. They hoped their action would inspire others to speak out against the lies, the demonisation and the blatant hypocrisy they saw around them. They wouldn't shut up, they wouldn't sit down. They wouldn't be pushed around any more.

RUQAYA (*direct address*). We had a ladder, yeah. It was my dad's. He uses it to do the guttering. Had to drag it all the way there because the driver wouldn't let me on the bus with it. Knew it was gonna be cold so I had seconds at dinner. And sneaked some banana cake in my pocket. Eating keeps you warm.

XARA (*direct address*). No eyes of the state could intimidate them. They were like ghosts. *Phantoms.*

RUQAYA (*direct address*). We were like ninjas.

SABI (*direct address*). We weren't like ninjas.

XARA (*direct address*). The ladder only got us as high as the first floor so we had to use the drain pipe to climb up to the window.

RUQAYA (*direct address*). Can I just say, we didn't mean to break the window, yeah?

SABI (*direct address*). We didn't *have* to. The one above it was still open.

RUQAYA (*direct address, of* SABI). She managed to cut her hand. (*Direct address.*) Told her, there's your DNA dripping all over the floor.

XARA (*direct address*). Nothing compared to the *lifeblood* those people have been taking from us.

RUQAYA (*direct address*). We used torches so we didn't have to turn the lights on.

XARA (*direct address*). Might as well send a bat signal to the cops, right?

SABI (*direct address*). We searched everywhere. Every cupboard, every drawer.

RUQAYA (*direct address*). You know they've got a little kitchen back there? Found the good biscuits.

XARA (*direct address*). She didn't take any.

RUQAYA (*direct address*). Not one.

SABI (*direct address*). In the end I found Xara's phone on Nadia's desk.

XARA *is elated to be reunited with her phone.*

RUQAYA (*direct address*). Maybe should've checked there first.

SABI (*direct address*). I found a dustpan and brush and cleaned up the glass from the window.

RUQAYA (*direct address*). You see any other robbers doing shit like that?

XARA (*direct address*). It wasn't a robbery. We were just taking back what's ours.

SABI (*direct address*). We found our stories in a box file behind Nadia's desk.

XARA (*direct address*). Loads of them. One for every girl who'd come through.

RUQAYA (*direct address*). I found Farouk!

SABI (*direct address*). I found my poem about the pole star.

XARA (*direct address*). I found my application to be an ambassador for Safe Sisters... We found every single thing they had with *our* names.

SABI (*direct address*). We didn't talk about doing it beforehand, it's like we just...

RUQAYA (*direct address*). All had the same thought...

XARA (*direct address*). At the same time.

They burn each one of the papers.

RUQAYA (*direct address*). Wasn't like we were destroying them...

XARA (*direct address*). More like we were *reclaiming* them.

SABI (*direct address*). Wise girl once said – 'You can learn anything off by heart if it *speaks* to your heart.'

RUQAYA (*direct address*). Turns out I shouldn't have thrown all that shade on Nadia.

XARA (*direct address*). She didn't report the break-in or anything.

RUQAYA (*direct address*). Even though we...

They turn the blinds around to reveal the spray-painted words 'Abolish Prevent'.

(*Direct address*.) We wanted to tell you what happened, because if we don't, no one else will, right?

SABI (*direct address*). So this is a space for us to learn together, share everything we know.

RUQAYA (*direct address*). Workshops, skill shares, the lot.

XARA (*direct address*). And once you know everything, you're going to want to do something about it.

SABI (*direct address*). You're going to want to join us in Liberation Square this Saturday. Twelve thirty p.m. To make our voices heard.

XARA (*direct address*). First rule of sisterhood. You always have each others' backs.

RUQAYA (*direct address*). This is the hour, knowledge is power.

SABI (*direct address*). Because if we don't speak up, who will?

Ends.

A Nick Hern Book

Liberation Squares first published in Great Britain as a paperback original in 2024 by Nick Hern Books Limited, The Glasshouse, 49a Goldhawk Road, London W12 8QP, in association with Fifth Word, Nottingham Playhouse and Brixton House

Liberation Squares copyright © 2024 Sonali Bhattacharyya

Sonali Bhattacharyya has asserted her right to be identified as the author of this work

Cover photography by Mathushaa Sagthidas

Designed and typeset by Nick Hern Books, London
Printed in Great Britain by Mimeo Ltd, Huntingdon, Cambridgeshire PE29 6XX

A CIP catalogue record for this book is available from the British Library

ISBN 978 1 83904 335 2

www.nickhernbooks.co.uk/environmental-policy

www.nickhernbooks.co.uk

facebook.com/nickhernbooks

twitter.com/nickhernbooks